Systematic, Sequential Vocabulary Development

WORDLY WISE 3000®

Cheryl Dressler, EdD
Illustrated by Bryan Langdo, Hannah Bureau, and Jannie Ho

Book 1

EDUCATORS PUBLISHING SERVICE
Cambridge and Toronto

Acquisitions/Development: Kate Moltz
Editor: Laura A. Woollett
Executive Editor: Bonnie Lass
Senior Designer: Karen Lomigora
Illustrators: Bryan Langdo, Hannah Bureau, and Jannie Ho

Printed in Canada

ISBN: 0-8388-2819-1
978-0-8388-2819-9

1 2 3 4 5 TRN 11 10 09 08 07

Dear Boys and Girls,

Welcome to Wordly Wise 3000 Book 1!

Your teacher will read you some stories and help you do some activities, too. You will learn lots of new words.

Have fun!

Story Words

leap

swamp

trunk

capital

monument

steep

load

globe

coast

nation

Directions: Have children look at the pictures as you read the story aloud.
Then have them mark items in the pictures related to **leap, swamp, trunk, capital,** and **monument.**

Directions: Have children number the pictures in the order they happened.

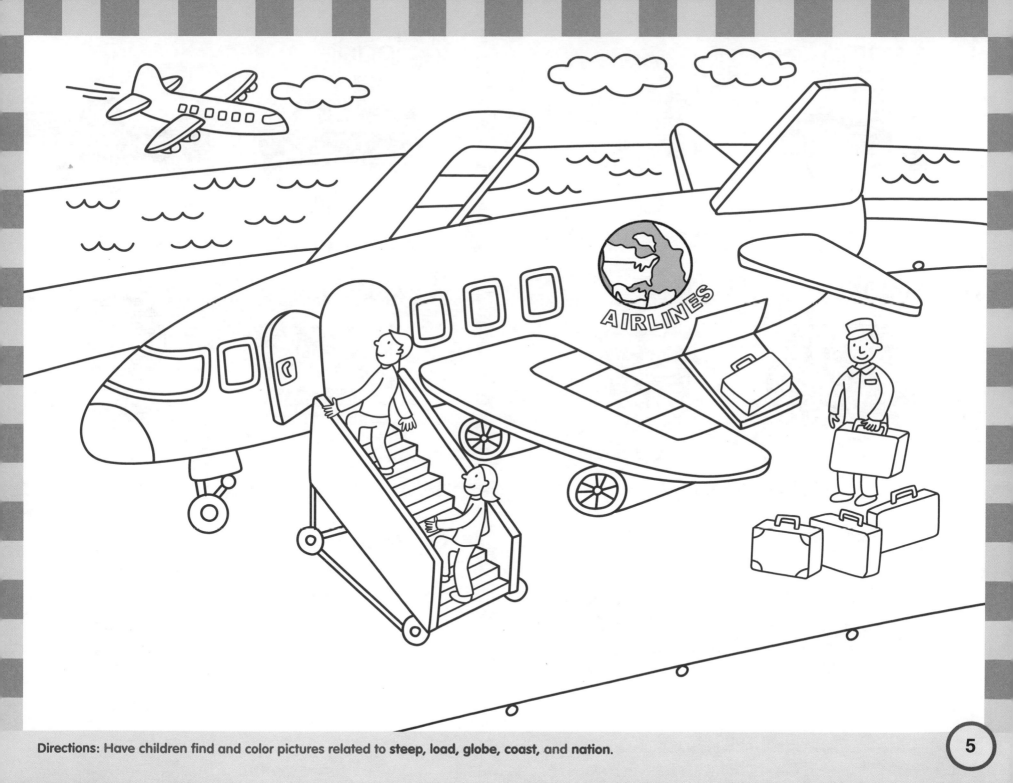

1. swamp

 ◯   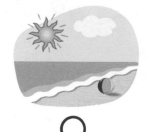 ◯

2. load

 ◯   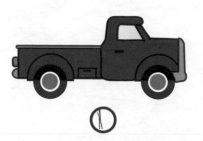 ◯

3. trunk

 ◯   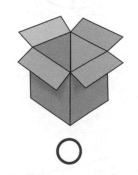 ◯

4. globe

 ◯    ◯

5. steep

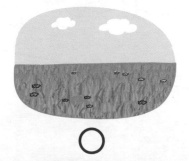 ◯    ◯

6. leap

 ◯    ◯

Directions: Have children fill in the bubble under the picture that matches the word you say.

Directions: Have children connect the **monuments**.

Story Words

peak

liquid

shallow

dip

compass

clear

flash

paddle

swift

wild

Directions: Have children look at the pictures as you read the story aloud.
Then have them mark items in the pictures related to **peak, liquid, shallow, dip,** and **compass.**

Directions: Have children number the pictures in the order they happened.

Directions: Have children find and color pictures related to **clear**, **flash**, **paddle**, **swift**, and **wild**.

1. clear

○ ○

2. wild

○ ○

3. shallow

○ ○

4. liquid

○ ○

5. swift

○ ○

6. peak

○ ○

Directions: Have children fill in the bubble under the picture that matches the word you say.

Directions: Have children use a yellow crayon to connect the things that **flash** and a red crayon to connect the things that are **wild**.

13

What Do You Know?

1. trunk

○ ○

2. flash

○ ○

3. dip

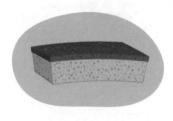 

○ ○

4. steep

 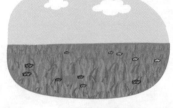

○ ○

5. globe

○ ○

6. compass

○ ○

Directions: Have children fill in the bubble under the picture that matches the word you say.

Journal

I Love you teacher.

Directions: Have children draw pictures of camping activities. Help them label their pictures.

15

Story Words

desert

bend

stump

temperature

dusk

enormous

decay

volcano

skeleton

prehistoric

Directions: Have children look at the pictures as you read the story aloud.
Then have them mark items in the pictures related to **desert, bend, stump, temperature,** and **dusk.**

Directions: Have children number the pictures in the order they happened.

Directions: Have children find and color pictures related to **enormous, decay, volcano, skeleton,** and **prehistoric.**

19

1. desert

 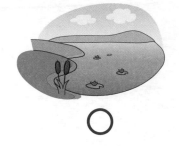
○ ○

2. dusk

○ ○

3. stump

○ ○

4. skeleton

○ ○

5. volcano

○ ○

6. prehistoric

○ ○

Directions: Have children fill in the bubble under the picture that matches the word you say.

Directions: Have children use a green crayon to connect the things that are **enormous** and a red crayon to connect the things that **bend**.

21

What Do You Know?

1. peak

○ ○

2. wild

○ ○

3. decay

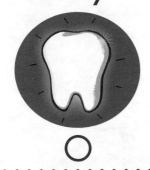 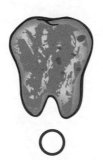

○ ○

4. temperature

○ ○

5. volcano

○ ○

6. clear

 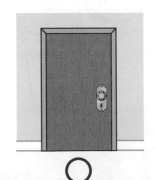

○ ○

Directions: Have children fill in the bubble under the picture that matches the word you say.

Journal

Directions: Have children illustrate and label the word **swamp, coast, peak, desert,** or **volcano.**

1

Story Words

thick

utensils

solid

separate

uneven

close

flaky

shape

boil

sprinkle

Directions: Have children look at the pictures as you read the story aloud.
Then have them mark items in the pictures related to **thick, utensils, solid, separate,** and **uneven.**

Directions: Have children number the pictures in the order they happened.

Directions: Have children find and color pictures related to **close**, **flaky**, **shape**, **boil**, and **sprinkle**.

27

1. separate

○ ○

2. boil

○ ○

3. flaky

○ ○

4. sprinkle

○ ○

5. thick

○ ○

6. uneven

○ ○

Directions: Have children fill in the bubble under the picture that matches the word you say.

Directions: Have children connect the **utensils**.

What Do You Know?

1. solid

○ ○

2. enormous

○ ○

3. bend

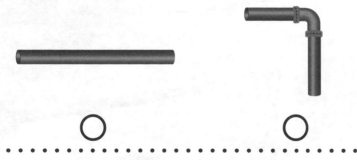

○ ○

4. close

○ ○

5. separate

○ ○

6. skeleton

○ ○

Directions: Have children fill in the bubble under the picture that matches the word you say.

Journal

Directions: Have children draw something they'd like to cook. Help them label their pictures.

Story Words

sway

property

arrange

rusty

attach

design

stormy

batteries

section

raise

Directions: Have children look at the pictures as you read the story aloud.
Then have them mark items in the pictures related to **sway, property, arrange, rusty,** and **attach.**

Directions: Have children number the pictures in the order they happened.

Directions: Have children find and color pictures related to **design**, **stormy**, **batteries**, **section**, and **raise**.

1. raise

○ ○

2. attach

○ ○

3. section

 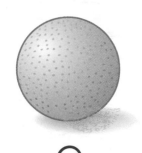

○ ○

4. arrange

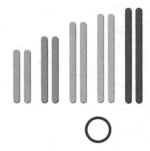 

○ ○

5. stormy

○ ○

6. sway

○ ○

Directions: Have children fill in the bubble under the picture that matches the word you say.

Directions: Have children connect the toys that are **rusty**.

What Do You Know?

1. attach

○　　　○

2. batteries

○　　　○

3. utensil

○　　　○

4. uneven

○　　　○

5. design

○　　　○

6. thick

○　　　○

Directions: Have children fill in the bubble under the picture that matches the word you say.

Journal

Directions: Have children draw a **design** for a room they would like to have. Help them label their designs.

Story Words

meet

cranky

train

injured

hatch

reverse

exhibit

misty

tropical

surface

Directions: Have children look at the pictures as you read the story aloud.
Then have them mark items in the pictures related to **meet**, **cranky**, **train**, **injured**, and **hatch**.

Directions: Have children number the pictures in the order they happened.

Directions: Have children find and color pictures related to **reverse**, **exhibit**, **misty**, **tropical**, and **surface**.

1. exhibit

◯ ◯

2. reverse

◯ ◯

3. surface

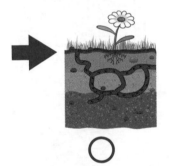 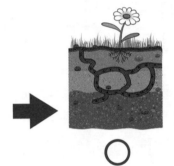

◯ ◯

4. cranky

◯ ◯

5. hatch

◯ ◯

6. train

◯ ◯

44

Directions: Have children fill in the bubble under the picture that matches the word you say.

Directions: Have children use a red crayon to connect the things that are **tropical** and a purple crayon to connect the things that are **misty**.

What Do You Know?

1. injured

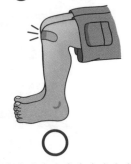 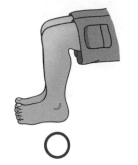

○ ○

2. stormy

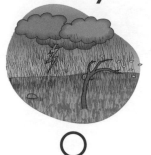 

○ ○

3. rusty

○ ○

4. surface

○ ○

5. meet

○ ○

6. raise

○ ○

Journal

Directions: Have children draw a **tropical** place and label it.

47

Story Words

cross

wagon

weave

fancy

tame

lively

chore

pile

ripe

hollow

Directions: Have children look at the pictures as you read the story aloud.
Then have them mark items in the pictures related to **cross, wagon, weave, fancy,** and **tame.**

2

3

Directions: Have children number the pictures in the order they happened.

Directions: Have children find and color pictures related to **lively**, **chore**, **pile**, **ripe**, and **hollow**.

1. weave

○ ○

2. pile

○ ○

3. cross

○ ○

4. hollow

○ ○

5. fancy

○ ○

6. wagon

○ ○

Directions: Have children fill in the bubble under the picture that matches the word you say.

Directions: Have children connect the kids who are doing **chores**.

What Do You Know?

1. lively

○   ○

2. misty

○   ○

3. hatch

○   ○

4. tame

○   ○

5. ripe

○   ○

6. exhibit

○   ○

Directions: Have children fill in the bubble under the picture that matches the word you say.

Journal

Directions: Have children draw and label pictures showing the two meanings of **cross** or **weave**.

Story Words

perform

fan

bashful

costume

modern

switch

ancient

action

entire

whirl

Directions: Have children look at the pictures as you read the story aloud.
Then have them mark items in the pictures related to **perform, fan, bashful, costume,** and **modern.**

Directions: Have children number the pictures in the order they happened.

Directions: Have children find and color pictures related to **switch**, **ancient**, **action**, **entire**, and **whirl**.

1. bashful

 ◯

 ◯

2. perform

 ◯

 ◯

3. entire

 ◯

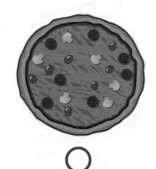 ◯

4. switch

 ◯

 ◯

5. whirl

 ◯

 ◯

6. fan

 ◯

 ◯

Directions: Have children fill in the bubble under the picture that matches the word you say.

Directions: Have children use a red crayon to connect the things that are **modern** and a purple crayon to connect the things that are **ancient**.

61

What Do You Know?

1. action

○ ○

2. fancy

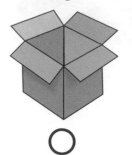 

○ ○

3. fan

○ ○

4. whirl

○ ○

5. weave

○ ○

6. hollow

○ ○

Directions: Have children fill in the bubble under the picture that matches the word you say.

Journal

Directions: Have children draw and label a picture of a **costume**.

Story Words

level

funnel

lean

object

reflect

fair

splendid

stake

remain

rapid

Directions: Have children look at the pictures as you read the story aloud.
Then have them mark items in the pictures related to **level, funnel, lean, object,** and **reflect.**

Directions: Have children number the pictures in the order they happened.

Directions: Have children find and color pictures related to **fair**, **splendid**, **stake**, **remain**, and **rapid.**

1. level

 ○    ○

2. splendid

 ○    ○

3. fair

 ○   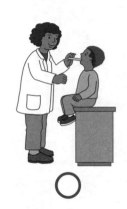 ○

4. funnel

 ○    ○

5. stake

 ○    ○

6. rapid

 ○    ○

Directions: Have children fill in the bubble under the picture that matches the word you say.

Directions: Have children use a red crayon to connect the things that **reflect** and a purple crayon to connect the things that are **leaning**.

69

What Do You Know?

1. remain

○ ○

2. modern

○ ○

3. entire

 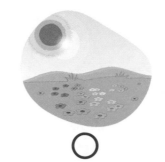

○ ○

4. fair

○ ○

5. object

○ ○

6. costume

○ ○

Journal

Directions: Have children draw and label a picture of something they think is **splendid**.

Story Words

filthy

motion

spray

hang

tank

scratch

entrance

vehicle

brakes

remove

1

Directions: Have children look at the pictures as you read the story aloud.
Then have them mark items in the pictures related to **filthy, motion, spray, hang,** and **tank.**

Directions: Have children number the pictures in the order they happened.

1. scratch

○   ○

2. tank

○   ○

3. vehicle

○   ○

4. entrance

○   ○

5. spray

○   ○

6. hang

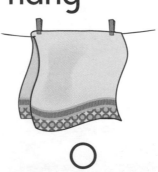

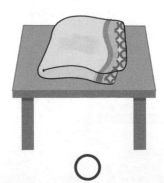

○   ○

Directions: Have children fill in the bubble under the picture that matches the word you say.

Directions: Have children connect the things that are **filthy**.

What Do You Know?

1. motion

○ ○

2. reflect

○ ○

3. level

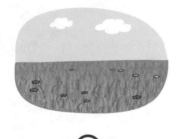 

○ ○

4. brakes

○ ○

5. stake

○ ○

6. remove

○ ○

Directions: Have children fill in the bubble under the picture that matches the word you say.

Journal

Directions: Have children use their imaginations to design and label a new kind of **vehicle**.

79

1

Story Words

headlight

pattern

caution

alone

gleaming

eager

adjust

steady

exercise

complete

Directions: Have children look at the pictures as you read the story aloud.
Then have them mark items in the pictures related to **headlight, pattern, caution, alone,** and **gleaming.**

2

3

Directions: Have children number the pictures in the order they happened.

Directions: Have children find and color pictures related to **eager**, **adjust**, **steady**, **exercise**, and **complete**.

1. pattern

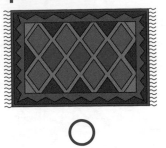 

○ ○

2. alone

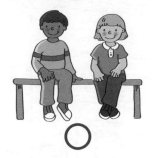 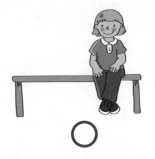

○ ○

3. complete

○ ○

4. gleaming

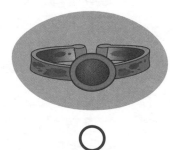 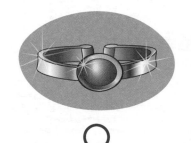

○ ○

5. eager

○ ○

6. steady

○ ○

84

Directions: Have children fill in the bubble under the picture that matches the word you say.

Directions: Have children connect the people who are exercising.

What Do You Know?

1. scratch

○ ○

2. caution

 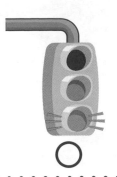

○ ○

3. adjust

○ ○

4. spray

○ ○

5. tank

 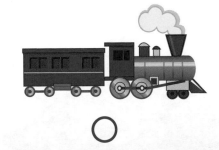

○ ○

6. headlight

○ ○

Directions: Have children fill in the bubble under the picture that matches the word you say.

Journal

Directions: Have children draw a **pattern** and label it.

Story Words

chart

button

view

land

tearful

whole

astronaut

dim

scale

tilt

Directions: Have children look at the pictures as you read the story aloud.
Then have them mark items in the pictures related to **chart, button, view, land,** and **tearful.**

Directions: Have children number the pictures in the order they happened.

Directions: Have children find and color pictures related to **whole**, **astronaut**, **dim**, **scale**, and **tilt**.

91

1. whole

◯   ◯

2. dim

◯   ◯

3. tilt

◯   ◯

4. land

◯   ◯

5. tearful

◯   ◯

6. chart

◯   ◯

Directions: Have children fill in the bubble under the picture that matches the word you say.

Directions: Have children use a green crayon to connect the things with **buttons** and a purple crayon to connect the things with **scales**.

93

What Do You Know?

1. view

○ ○

2. pattern

○ ○

3. exercise

○ ○

4. land

○ ○

5. astronaut

○ ○

6. steady

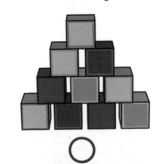 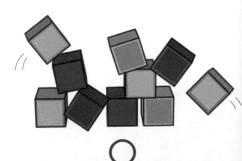
○ ○

Directions: Have children fill in the bubble under the picture that matches the word you say.

Journal

Directions: Have children draw a **view** from a space shuttle. Help them label their drawings.

Story Words

awkward

tide

construct

tower

drop

bold

divide

equal

length

receive

Directions: Have children look at the pictures as you read the story aloud.
Then have them mark items in the picture related to **awkward, tide, construct, tower,** and **drop.**

2

3

Directions: Have children number the pictures in the order they happened.

Directions: Have children find and color pictures related to **bold, divide, equal, length,** and **receive.**

1. tower

○ ○

2. divide

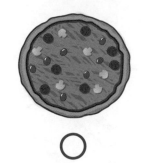 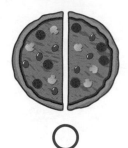
○ ○

3. bold

○ ○

4. drop

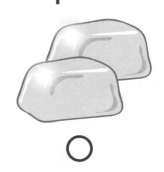 
○ ○

5. construct

○ ○

6. tide

○ ○

Directions: Have children fill in the bubble under the picture that matches the word you say.

Directions: Have children connect the pairs of shapes that are **equal** in size.

What Do You Know?

1. awkward

◯ ◯

2. tearful

◯ ◯

3. length

◯ ◯

4. receive

◯ ◯

5. scale

◯ ◯

6. button

◯ ◯

Directions: Have children fill in the bubble under the picture that matches the word you say.

Journal

Directions: Have children draw and label a picture of a favorite gift they have **received**.

103

Story Words

simple

rude

wind

sob

damaged

meadow

atmosphere

crash

search

clever

Directions: Have children look at the pictures as you read the story aloud.
Then have them mark items in the picture related to **simple, rude, wind, sob,** and **damaged.**

GRADE 1 IS #1

Directions: Have children number the pictures in the order they happened.

1. simple

○   ○

2. atmosphere

○   ○

3. crash

○   ○

4. search

○   ○

5. damaged

○   ○

6. wind

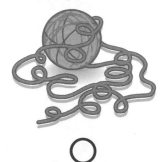 

○   ○

Directions: Have children fill in the bubble under the picture that matches the word you say.

Directions: Have children use a red crayon to connect pictures that demonstrate the word **rude** and a purple crayon to connect pictures that demonstrate the word **clever**.

What Do You Know?

1. meadow

 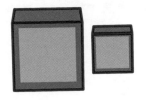

○   ○

2. equal

○   ○

3. drop

○   ○

4. sob

○   ○

5. divide

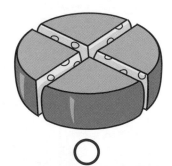 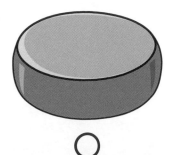

○   ○

6. wind

○   ○

Directions: Have children fill in the bubble under the picture that matches the word you say.

Journal

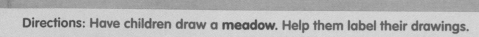

Directions: Have children draw a **meadow.** Help them label their drawings.

111

1

Story Words

month

mural

imitate

applause

photograph

grow

rise

mature

memory

artistic

Directions: Have children look at the pictures as you read the story aloud.
Then have them mark items in the picture related to **month, mural, imitate, applause,** and **photograph.**

Directions: Have children number the pictures in the order they happened.

Journal

Directions: Have children draw a **memory** from first grade. Help them label their pictures.

My Word Lists

These pages are here for you to collect words. They can be words you learned in the stories in this book, or they can be other words you know. Each page has a subject at the top that tells you what kinds of words to write. There is also a page for you to write any words you want.

Places

Caroline, Jordan, and Maggie have visited many places. What places have you visited? Where would you like to go? Write names of places and words about places here.

Jobs

You have read about a baker, a builder, and a zookeeper. What jobs do you know about? Which job would you like to have? Write names of jobs here.

Special Days

The kids in Ms. Shuman's class learned all about New Year's celebrations. New Year's is a special day. What days are special to you? Write names of special days here.

Transportation

Cars, bikes, and airplanes are all kinds of transportation. What ways do you know to get from one place to another? Write transportation words here.

Art

The kids in Ms. Shuman's class know all about art! Caroline built a sand castle, and everyone made kites and a big mural. What kinds of art do you like? Write art words here.

My Favorite Words

Words are everywhere! Write your favorite words here.